The Day Somebody Offered Me the Moon

By Sandra C. Maineri

Dedication:

To all my mentors, friends and inspirational poets.

My Mom and Dad, Claire and Sando Bologna, Mom loved poetry and Dad loved seeing my work published early on.

My sisters, Anita Bologna and Flavia Johnston DePolo, enthusiastic supporters.

Alberta Maineri-Burke, Terese Louise Maineri de Velasquez and Kristi Lyn Sadosky- doting daughters and fodder for the pen.

My sons-in-law, Dr. Michael Burke, who lights the fire to my motivation, Mateo Velasquez Lopez for introducing me to Guatemala and Eric, our newest poetry fan

My grandchildren, Gabe, Matty, Alberto, Mateo, Clara-Louise, Christopher and Sandra. They inspire me and I hope I inspire them.

Melanie Gundy for the cover design.

Special thanks to Lorna Morris Cyr, a true friend and mentor.

Marie Sassi for a well-appreciated endorsement, educator, poet.

Nikki Giovanni, poet extraordinaire.

John Ciardi, author of my favorite poem.

Those aging Sisters of Mercy who valued traditional poetry.

Anna Granniss, whose poetic footsteps I would like to walk in.

Finally and foremost, my husband Al who supports and praises my efforts always.

Table of Contents

Full Moon Rising

The Day Somebody Offered Me the Moon

The day somebody offered

me the moon,

I was cleaning the bathroom

and couldn't comprehend the gesture.

I remember thinking

"A shooting star from time to

time would do"

but it was the moon or nothing.

The day somebody offered

me the moon,

the baby had a runny

nose, the ceiling leaked

and the car wouldn't start.

It was hard to put the

whole thing in perspective

But the moon looked

pretty good.

The day somebody offered

me the moon,

Daddy came home tired

and hungry, with tons

of papers to correct,

not in the mood to

hear about the deal.

The day somebody offered

me the moon,

I finally got my priorities

straight, shelved my tidbit

dilemmas, donned a

spacesuit, and flew away.

December Moon

For Sandy Hook

Wintery late-night luminary

shower us with moonbeams.

Crystal snowflakes catch your

Brightness.

We are drawn to you, like to the

Christmas star.

Celestial orb, revolving through

Heavens.

Hope- beacon on coldest night.

We search the sky for answers

to life's growing hoard of questions.

You know the

Why of things.

Your peacefulness never

wavers.

Those who pace in pre-dawn

frenzy,

Sleepless with sorrow

grieving, despondent

recognize your beauty,

challenge you to reveal

what is hidden behind

stars of night.

Little souls flutter by,

caught in moon-beam glow.

Unseen angels tapping lightly

with fragile wings.

Wishing, so much wishing, as

to create.

14

Sighing, so deep a sigh, as

to despair.

Yet moon, you shine on

lighting darkened hearts.

Keeping your mysteries,

embracing new cherubs.

Soul Mate

Did you pray for me,

when I was roaming

cock-eyed, through

the world?

Did you see through me

with laser eyes that pierced

my wandering soul?

Halting in your gaze,

I turn toward

those forever arms

and rush to kiss with

penitential reverence

your enduring smile.

A Gift

I'm wrapping up my life like a present,

hiding all the sweetness inside

taping edges gingerly

preventing essence, lost.

Inside, joy of childhood

gives way to adolescent yearnings

confused, confounded, shocked

at the bigger world,

sweet evolution to young romance.

Sincere vows, newness of

everything.

Perfection in a wink,

then-babies, rushing, no time

to breathe –

Years of peeling off old nail

polish.

17

Car needs work,

so do I.

Almost empty nest

Aging lovers holding hands, TV

popcorn- a game –

concerned, jaded shocked

at the bigger world.

No place for prayer, or Christmas

Crèche, political correctness- not so

correct.

Folding the last corner,

neatly, as if "wrapped up" was

better than opened,

as if to stay within the box a

bit longer.

I'm wrapping up my life

like people wrap up gifts.

I'm giving it to you.

Ode to an Indifferent Plant

I have watered you and talked to you.

And you stay safely potted, looking

for roots that don't exist, shrinking

from that which you could be.

And I can do no more for you,

than pluck the weeds.

You must transplant yourself.

I'm a climbing, not a clinging vine

and cannot bear to leave behind

one that has a bud, but will not bloom.

One living thing that will not grow.

Inspire

He steps out onto the wire

Two inches of reality amid chaos.

He knows the wire.

He's studied it since he was two.

He knows how to curl his toes

in soft suede boots to steady

his gait.

The crowd as deafening as

the falls is audible.

He listens to his father's

voice.

"One foot after another, vary

your rhythm," dad prompts.

Thirteen minutes into the

walk, he is above the

torrent, the thunder, the gorge.

Balancing poles leans first

left, then right.

Mighty gusts of wind surround him.

The falls do not embrace him.

He struggles on.

Half way across, visions

of his grandfather,

master of the wire, surface.

No time to reminisce

Concentrating step by step

above the swirly drop.

Cold mist slaps his face

reminding him.

There is wire in his blood.

He can see his wife's

outstretched arms, feel

his daughter's prayers,

he bends on one knee to

give thanks –

then dances, and

jumps to the waiting crowd.

Unwrapped passport,

he hands it to Canadian Mounties.

"Have you anything to declare?"

He declares nothing!

"What is the purpose of

your visit?" They inquire.

"TO INSPIRE,"

he replies.

Moon Beams & Lunar Craters

Yield

Nothing much happens at middle age,

except a pause.

Dreams fulfilled

or forgotten.

Kids growing

or grown.

Home half-yours,

half the bank's.

Your spouse blends into

a half-worn mattress

becomes a

comfortable mound.

You wish like hell something

great would stir you.

But you are set in your ways.

Half-way down

a one-way street.

Yo Yo

You don't even hold the string yet

I find myself winding back to you.

Sometimes skipping,

sometimes spinning,

sometimes rushing,

wildly into your waiting hands.

You hold me for an instant,

then gently make me fly.

I am free with you.

I am free because of you.

I am caught up and dangling

from a thread that can't be seen,

forever attached.

Honor Me

Honor me with your promises,

ones made when drunk with yearning,

uncontrolled emotion spilling into

unrelented passion.

Honor me with your promises,

not sweet, "*I love yous*" when you pass.

Walk with me, talk with me.

Be with me what you were and

I will become more and more and more.

A sweet line of praise, a tender grasp, a laugh

with the flicker of lust remembered. Remember?

Honor me with your promises,

ones meant to last forever

till death or longer and

I will honor you.

To the Wind

Hang love-lanterns, shining bright,

'Mid gentle branches, moonlit night.

Paste petals on each fading rose.

Send sonnets filled with pleasant prose.

Dance while field flowers sway.

Embrace the wind, caress the day.

Keep hidden heart but wise reflection,

Joy with sorrow, lost perfection.

Store memories in spill proof tins.

Encourage love, not might have-beens.

Save symphonies of heartfelt laughter.

Whisper fast "forever after," to the wind.

Christmas, Age 2

I hid plastic Jesus 'neath the

tree.

Above hung Mickey Mouse and Snoopy

too.

And wandering to touch each shiny

ball.

Came our toddler, the way that

children do.

She eyed each ornament that

brightly gleamed, then

spied the Babe and knelt

to hold Him near.

"Can I kiss Him, and play

with Him?" she called.

I nodded, though I really didn't

hear.

"This is God," she smiled, "I

found Him – I want Pappa

and Bachi to see."

She alone had noticed

he'd been missing

Caught beneath the clutter

of the tree.

A Friendly Game of Cards

"Mothering is not my strongest suit,"

she said, leading with her heart.

He had bid in diamonds,

she accepted. They had joined the club.

Now, afraid to deal, she watched the game.

Unshuffled cards fell slowly from her hands.

She would have no part of jokers.

She would not wait for spades.

Instead, she prayed that

hearts would once again be trump.

Alberta Clipper

You rattle me, Alberta Clipper

blowing in from the Northwest.

Wind at your heels,

Hair set free to frame your

Face,

Hips hugged in "hot" jeans.

Shoes for running.

I see you embrace the

Statue of Liberty.

Welcome newcomers,

speak their words,

eat their food!

Flowing with the fickle

breath of fall,

you dance on

swirling leaves.

Racing the running dog

to find you're home again.

You're home again

and then you're not.

You rattle me Alberta Clipper.

Circadian Rhythms

The Color Ignorant

Ah ha! A new shade of stupid,

the color ignorant.

It stands out in a room, blends

poorly with everything,

is rarely subdued.

Clashes with reason,

common sense and good taste,

always provokes comments,

seldom goes unnoticed.

Is more prevalent in spring

brings out your worse features

Have you noticed a lot of

people wearing it lately?

Mime Time

Applause Marcel Marceau,

master of mime.

We live with your fantasies

part of the time.

Pushing against invisible walls

leaning on make-believe ledges,

tripping over unobserved obstacles.

We are actors on a silent screen.

Each allowed one silent scream

and a chance to mimic

vague realities.

Applause. Applause, Marcel Marceau

You lend us the faces.

You teach us the moves.

You hold our props when

we are not on stage.

Irish Minstrel

Irish Minstrel at the Heart

Crisp chinz skirts fly in straight lines

across stage.

Soft feet in softer shoes, stomp

in sweet precision.

Banshee wails fill the air.

Drums, flutes, strings join in

"The Rising of the Moon."

A single shaky tenor questions:

"Does your mother come

From Ireland?" and "Sweet

Molly Malone"

No Celtic women here!

Freckled faces under make up

Reel again

While green and white striped skirts

Fly like flag of Erin

The audience rises to its feet

They always do while the last

song plays

"Soldiers are we whose

lives are pledged to Ireland"

I didn't know till I was 50 –

It's Ireland's national anthem

I just thought- "St. Patrick's Day

A standing O.

They liked the show."

Balloon

Life,

like a child's first

balloon, is high and

bright and swiftly slips

through unknowing

fingers.

4 O'clock

English Tea –

Steeped in

tradition.

Like Quilts

Some friends are like

familiar quilts guaranteed to

cover you with warm feeling.

Some have faded little by little

over the years.

They are thread-bare in

need of repair, barely together.

Others look none the worse for

wear.

I admit not caring enough for

them,

not choosing to be covered by

their warmth, I've put them

away.

46

But now, they are in tatters,

almost impossible to patch.

I can't discard them.

The Weaver

Never have I strung the loom,

nor held the shuttle,

weaver though I am.

Many threads collected

Arranged one by one.

Pull close, hold fast, release.

Variegated, twisted specks

patterned in their way

amaze me!

Pull close, hold fast, release.

The piece not yet complete,

the garment never worn,

the pace ebbs and flows.

Pull close, hold fast, release.

Work of my own hands,

unlike another.

Thread for thread, I know you.

Jacquard pattern,

I have woven you to

stand the test of time.

Blue Moon

Assault on the Sea

Troop out the colors, the tide's

in retreat. March out of the

marshes, the brown naked feet.

To the edge of the waves and

then some we go.

The sea will surrender,

its surf is so slow. Call back

the marchers, sound the alarm,

the tide is attacking.

The sea means to harm.

Through ripples of waves

and soft shifting sand, run

to the marshes, as fast as you can.

An army so weary hasn't a chance

to ward off the waves with its tired dance.

Pick up the sea rolls, run from the foam.

Tell all the naked feet, time to march home.

In the morning, at low tide, we'll plan an attack.

Tell the sea to be ready, we're all coming back.

Meig's Point

For Alberto

People have come here

for solace, undisturbed calm.

For memories tossed like

crashing waves.

Looking down, among

the shells, weathered, not

broken, I take comfort.

Looking up at white

gulls bantering, I feel spirit.

Ocean sprays

mists. Sand and stones

leave sparkling crystals.

Penguin people in

winter coats rock slowly

along the jetty for a

closer moment with

the sea.

There is nothing here

really,

Water you can't drink,

Sand instead of soil.

There is nothing here,

except everything.

I am drawn to it,

I must return.

April Afternoons

I fell under the spell of the sun

melting into April afternoons,

blending with the garden soil,

growing with spring seeds.

Bursting out of hidden winter bulbs

come tulips, daffodils.

Up from deep furrows

shoot bashful peony,

leaping inches overnight.

In the middle,

I am growing some,

not bursting nor leaping

just pushing through enough

to catch the warming rays.

Down to the River

Way into July it takes the

sycamore, the lazy sycamore

To unfurl its foliage.

Finally, half-naked trunk,

Shielded in green leaves

Tall, old, proud tree.

Who sat on this bank before

us?

Who waded river with

doe and fawn?

Keeper of secrets, you know

who left the half-read book and

empty cup.

You know whose little

feet marched proudly to

water's edge.

You are shelter in summer rain

beauty in autumn,

solemnity in winter,

But you are most yourself

now, bursting forth in

lavish leaves to shade our

bench, to welcome yellow finches.

Autumn Released

The first hard freeze has come

but leaves linger in precarious poses

unwilling to yield.

Hardy mums speak volumes in their

silence.

Splendid pompons hold their ground.

Yesterday's pumpkins form tender

mush in late afternoon sun.

Frantic squirrel buries his stash,

scrambles to forage again.

Seasoned logs stand split and ready.

Damp, frosty air gathers in

north to chill ground,

heralding the hint of frost

Still, leaves will not yield.

Vibrating in even harsher winds,

they dare not leap-

for fear of being gathered

for fear of being burned.

The last of holding on.

The grasp of branch

of breath

of life,

Sweet moments in the breeze,

Echoes of picnics,

sheltered by oak's prayerful,

arms –

61

And then unexpectedly

they fall, swirl, pivot,

lie motionless on fading grass.

Testament to nature's edicts,

Autumn Released.

Hanging On

Maple leaf, caught in spider's web

      dance the wind, dance,

      throb to thunder's tune.

Flash rust – brown with

      lightning speed

      sway lightly in the foggy grey dawn.

How perfect your shape,

      pointed herald of fall.

Veins, direct droplets down

      slender stem, dripping on

      beetle caught in web.

Sheets of runoff wash away

      summer grime,

      set the glass for sun light.

Still you hold on tightly,

       shaken but undisturbed.

I would keep you, as a

       testament to August,

       gentle gymnast,

       one of thousands, tumbling

       from the trees.

Only one wise enough

       to choose the web and window,

       to state a claim to winter's immortality,

I shall not disturb you.

Harvest Moon

Easter Bread

It is not gentle pushing

which gives way to desperate kneading

nor smell of fresh ground nutmeg-

mixed with yeast

nor sweet aroma of bread rising.

It is not golden color

glazed in egg.

Nor lingering flavor

of twist braided loaf.

It is not holiness of season.

Nor ritual of creating.

It is not newness of Spring.

Nor joy of Easter.

It is you, Grandmother.

Noni Cookies

They are Noni cookies.

Brown biscotti-like confections.

Cousin brought some to the house.

Hers were plain and dry,

lacking the orange zest I add to mine

They had a texture, a telltale

texture that said "organic"

good for you graham flour,

raw sugar –

They are cookies!

They don't have to be

good for you!

They require little hands

reaching for the cookie box,

like Alberto does when he visits me,

like I did when I was little

and visited Noni to watch her

roll the dough.

No recipe in sight.

I realize now, she could not read.

No measuring cups –

she used her hands.

They remained the same size.

The cookies were always the same:

perfect.

Then there is the thing about

the nuts, neatly, evenly placed in

each.

Cousin must have forgotten.

I never do - cookies or not.

You've got to have nuts

They are everywhere.

They make life interesting.

I put her batch on the

porch and made some of

my own –

"Don't you love Noni cookies?"

she remarked when leaving.

"I do" I said, I do.

Late Night with Ben & Jerry

I've been eating ice cream again

out of the box.

My dirty little late night indulgence

savoring its flavor

rolling it around on my tongue

numbing my lips and jaw.

I feel the muscles in my face relax,

musing in the dark

thinking how good chocolate

tastes when it's cold.

There are only two of us now

in the house, and the dog.

It won't stay a secret long.

Little spoon tracks on

the bottom of the box

begin to show,

Half-empty and never been served.

Climbing into bed, my mind

numb as my mouth.

Guiltless till tomorrow.

I slumber till rising sun,

Content

with a delicious smile on

my face.

Lunar Eclipse

Zapatos

Her feet are Guatemalan,

Brown like the dusty roads they tread.

Brown like his face and his hands.

Mayan-brown, clay and corn

setting sun mid sunflowers.

Her feet are Guatemalan.

They know the way thru winding

paths from Santiago to Pascal,

children chase soccer balls and each other.

Her feet are Guatemalan,

Sandal-clad on rocky roads

swiftly paced on cobblestones,

Antigua in the fall.

Her feet are Guatemalan.

They step through burning candles

in iglesia Santa Domingo.

Flower petals and white rum,

honor the Virgin on her feast day.

All the Guatemalan feet.

follow in procession, drums banging, fireworks flying,

abuelos chanting in praise of Mary, in thanks for

simple blessings, in joy and sorrow,

on narrow roads with Guatemalan feet.

Wedding in Guatemala

When I ran into bowl of twenty-six turkey heads

while searching for running water,

they all had that shaken look on their faces.

"Why here? Why now? Why me?

Wedding guests, unaware of their plight

feasted on the rest of them,

Licking luscious fingers, dipping, grabbing

with hot tortillas, mixing with mixed rice.

Laughing, licking, luscious and when

they cleared away the carcasses and dance floor,

the thump of shrill donkeys wailed from the

Marimba band and I merged with the traffic

going right, thinking all the while,

"Why here? Why now? Why me?

Bubbles – age 2 –

He delights in bubbles

grabbing, reaching

screeching, shrieking,

unabashed joy

Laughing, jumping, leaping

for iridescent spheres

which rise, float

disintegrate – no remains

save a tiny spot on

wooden floor.

The smell of clean, fresh

light bubbles,

"bubbles, bubbles

big big bubbles

dip dip daddy – blow."

Dance in the delight- of the day.

In Orbit

Equation

My aloneness is panic plus

infinity, forever.

My apartness the next

universe but farther.

My longings I can neither

count nor multiply.

Innumerable joys divided by

endless sorrow equals

nothing.

For My Own Loss

I went to a wake today,

you were not invited.

It was a wake for one,

to bury parts of me that

have been dying,

dented dreams, ruptured

smiles and a major

slice of soul.

I went to a wake today,

to mourn my own passing.

Not grieving over lost limbs,

but more regretting forfeited

identity, a little like Samson

staring at his heap of hair and

manhood, quickly cut away.

I went to a wake today.

It was brief, unreligious,

hardly an event to be remembered.

Yet I had that funeral feeling.

I cried for my own loss.

Your Poem

Should I climb slowly from

this abyss,

I do so with your poem in hand.

Hope lifts wary, wandering thoughts

of separation and despair.

You are there, thinking only good

thoughts,

So simple, so profound.

Gesture of love

Spark to unlit flame,

Warmth in winter.

If I climb out from this abyss,

you are there

waiting to be with me.

Assisted Living

He rises to his feet wrapped in lamb's wool.

They move, one slowly following the other.

Like the letter "Z" in slow motion

bent at the hips, leaning hard one way,

bent at the chest and pushing head-on

down the hall.

Blue/gray eyes searching

through their cloudy lenses.

Slender bent hands reaching for a chair.

"I'm winded," he sighs.

That awful deep down sigh, squeezing

a melancholy moan in front of him.

There's a pause, then feet move,

one following the other, dragging

the boots behind him, he smiles.

The banana is in sight.

Cranberry cookies on the counter

beckon. A shaky grasp, a turn,

the hallway is as long as it ever was.

"*I'm hungry*," he smiles, reaching for

the door, his haven, his home,

his prison.

But I don't

I care not for you ole man,

teeth by side of the bed.

Walker strewn with crumpled clothes

commode in the corner.

Endless streams of nonsense songs

"Baa Baa Black Sheep."

The sunshine's bright while

the black becomes white,

"My Ole Kentucky Home,"

far away, far away,

You are far away, far away,

Papa, Papa, pickle-loving,

Get me an orange.

"Hey Albert, Hey Albert,

I need you,"

"Hey Albert, Hey Albert"

I need you too."

I do not care for you old man.

I care for you.

But I don't.

Get Well Soon

I put off calling you,

knowing you could help,

knowing you've been there for me.

Knowing I should have gone

and sought you out.

You could have at least held

back the pain, lessened it a bit.

Put a dent in my negative mind.

You would have made me feel better.

But I delayed, forgetting the past.

Thinking I could work things through,

put this terror behind me, toughen up.

Now, I feel for you in the dark,

praying you will be there where I left you,

waiting silently to be consumed.

I wrap my hands around you,

swallow hard and pray.

The Promise

Mother, rush! The summer

flowers are dying.

Quickly catch their petals

as they fall.

Winter winds will sweep

their shallow gravesites.

Will we, their gentle

fragrances recall?

Hush, my child, it's just

the seasons changing.

Do not mourn your vivid

visions gone.

Each flower springs a seed,

a new beginning,

The promise that life's sweet

bouquet goes on.

November Funeral

Tossing farewell flowers

on a copper coffin

in the rain.

Tented sorrows

on tear-soaked sod.

Puddles collect with thoughts

of far-away days.

November hangs so low,

gray and mournful.

It's hard to find blessings

for the '*Thanking Day*'.

There remain faded memories

floating slowly down

a grassy field,

Merging with an autumn mist.

95

Moon Walk

The Family Photo

Her eyes, her eyes show that

vacant look

that followed her thru life.

She stands slightly behind her husband,

hand on the back of his chair.

He sits stern and stately in

buttoned down vest and matching

suit, open-necked shirt

one hand around cocky little

Louis,

who stands by papa's chair

one hand on hip, one on Papa's

knee.

Even in his knickers, he claims

his place in the family.

Older sister in white dress

only dress, with large white bows

in her hair (you have to know she was pretty) –

leans her elbow lightly on Papa's

forearm.

Brother Frank, oldest boy,

In sailor suit matching Louie's –

He is firmly planted in front of

Mama.

He is safe there and happy.

He does not wish to leave her side.

He will stay with her his

entire life.

Missing is little Lawrence.

He would have been 5.

But it is 1911 a fragile

Lawrence did not survive

diphtheria.

"Did you want a photo, ma'am?"
a photographer asked. He came to
their house to memorialize the little
guy in the coffin.
"No no" Mama replied, "He was
so busy, so happy. This is not him"
Victoria would tell this story
well into her 80s, stopping each
time to brush away tears.

"Mama would look out the
kitchen window for hours," she added.
Regina would retire her crisp white
blouse and black skirt in preference
for black dresses, after baby
Emma died suddenly – She was
only 40 days old.

Then there was Albert,

beloved last son, gentle loving

Albert.

Regina was too weary by 1913

to ever pay serious attention to

her brood.

Her eyes became more hollow

as her memories disintegrated.

Louie kept his room, a claim

to the ole' homestead.

Frank stayed too, marrying

Josephine and raising their 2 children

there.

Albert built a home down the

street. He brought his mom

the Italian newspaper on his

way home from work.

Victoria married and moved to Meriden.

By then Papa, tyrant in

residence, had passed away.

The old homestead revealed

imperfections of half-lives lived.

It stood unchanged until the '90s

when it was converted to a condo.

The farm fields were filled in

with neat little other matching homes.

Papa, Mama, Frank, Louie and

Vicky, long gone-

Albert, last to pass, left his

memories before he left this

place.

Still surrounded in ornate

silver frame the family remains.

Papa and 3 of the 6 moody

well-dressed kids vie for a

key spot in the photo-

Regina, somewhat apart is

already fading, fading, fading.

Larabee Plays Chopin's First

I waited.

No hint of piano.

He sat motionless,

Shock of white hair hid his face.

Then those first few notes

that tickle and tease

that gentle piano rain,

descending softly, softly unmistakably.

Not a sound, save his genius,

merged with genius.

He leaned into it,

allowed it to take him

fell into it, like a drowning

sailor unable, or unwilling to

grasp the life float,

carried away

swiftly by the undercurrent

of the piece.

Fingering each note,

like touching a newborn baby for the

first time,

reverence, holiness, allegro, joyfulness.

Violins hasten to keep up,

Conductor digs deep,

nods to soloist

audience leans in to sop up

each final note

like bread in an empty

soup bowl- wanting more.

He stands,

They stand.

He is gone, returns, gone,

leaving half-notes of the genius

still dancing in the air.

If I could love

someone from the past, it

would be Chopin, for all he gave,

but I would still want to hug Larabee.

End of the Storm

--for Kylie—

Do not fear flash of light

Pangs of panic, thunderclash.

Desperation of the night

Daylight dawns at last.

I am there, strong as thunder

Bright as lightning in the sky.

I am there in joy and wonder

to kiss away each tear you cry.

By your side at every turn

quiet wisdom to share.

By your side when you yearn

for me, I am there, I am there.

Wisdom of the ages rests within your heart,

listen as it beats your tune.

We are not apart.

We meet again mid stars and moon,

a universe beyond.

I am here, now

I am here.

"Sandra Maineri's poems in her new collection, "The Day Somebody Offered Me The Moon," are filled with compassion, joys, sorrows and the humor of a life fully lived. The poem "Soul Mate," offering lines, 'did you pray for me when I was roaming cock-eyed through the world' wonderfully bears this out. There is intellect and a depth of truth in this book."

—Maria Sassi, award winning poet and playwright, author of "Rooted in Stars," "Rare Grasses," and "What I see," a prize-winning chapbook of ekphrastic poems.

Made in the USA
Middletown, DE
15 April 2021